Sports Illustrated
TRAINING
WITH
WEIGHTS

The Sports Illustrated Library

BOOKS ON TEAM SPORTS

Baseball	Football: Defense	Ice Hockey
Basketball	Football: Offense	Pitching
Curling: Techniques and Strategy	Football: Quarterback	Soccer
		Volleyball

BOOKS ON INDIVIDUAL SPORTS

Badminton	Horseback Riding	Table Tennis
Fly Fishing	Judo	Tennis
Golf	Skiing	Track: Field Events
Handball	Squash	Track: Running Events
		Wrestling

BOOKS ON WATER SPORTS

Powerboating	Small Boat Sailing
Skin Diving and Snorkeling	Swimming and Diving

SPECIAL BOOKS

Dog Training   Training with Weights
Safe Driving

Sports Illustrated
TRAINING WITH WEIGHTS

By ROBERT B. PARKER
and JOHN R. MARSH

Photographs
by Michael Louridas

J. B. LIPPINCOTT COMPANY
New York

U.S. Library of Congress Cataloging in Publication Data

Parker, Robert B   birth date
  Sports illustrated training with weights

(Sports illustrated library)
  1. Weight lifting.   I. Marsh, John R.,
birth date   II. Title.
GV546.P29   1974   796.4'1   73-9817
ISBN-0-397-01006-0
ISBN-0-397-01005-2 (pbk.)

Copyright © 1974, by Time Inc.
All rights reserved
Printed in the United States of America

81 82 83 84 85   15 14 13 12 11 10

Cover photograph: Michael Louridas

Contents

INTRODUCTION	9
1. NECK AND SHOULDERS	19
NECK	19
SHOULDERS	23
2. ARMS	36
UPPER-ARM BICEPS	36
UPPER-ARM TRICEPS	46
FOREARMS, WRISTS, HANDS	54
3. CHEST	57
4. BACK	66
5. WAIST	72
ABDOMEN	72
OBLIQUES	77

6. LEGS 81
    THIGHS 81
    CALVES 88

7. TRAINING PROGRAMS FOR THE BEGINNER 92

AN AFTERWORD ON PHYSICAL CONDITION 95

Sports Illustrated
TRAINING WITH WEIGHTS

Introduction

THERE IS A LOT of nonsense associated with weight training. Here are some samples:
(1) "If you lift weights, you'll get muscle-bound."
(2) "Once you start lifting weights, you can never stop."
(3) "Weight lifters are weirdos."

Most people who use the term muscle-bound don't know what it means. Neither do we. Advanced body builders like the ones on magazine covers may have a greater tendency toward muscle pulls, and excessive development of certain muscles may make some people *look* awkward (though not necessarily *be* awkward). These are exceptional circumstances, of concern only to people who work out with weights 5 or 6 hours a day. If someone tells you that you will get muscle-bound from weight training, ask him to explain exactly what he means by muscle-bound.

The assumption that once you begin weight training you must always continue is based on the assumption that the built-up muscle will turn to fat as soon as you stop exercising. That's not quite the way the body works. There is a good deal less known about obesity than there should be, but as far as anyone can tell, fatness and nonfatness depend on whether you take in more calories than you use up, or use up more calories than you take in. Thus, if you exercise vigorously every day and use up excess calories, your weight will stay stable. If you stop exercising and continue to eat the same amount, you will get fatter. If you reduce the amount you eat, to compensate for the reduction in the amount you use up, you won't get fatter. Or if you substitute, say, swimming for weight lifting and burn up the same number of calories, you won't get fatter. What does happen when you stop lifting weights is that the muscles which were hard get flabby. But you will be no flabbier than you would be if you had never exercised with weights in the first place. We don't wish to oversimplify a complicated business (the relationship between weight, fat, exercise and diet), but this is true—you can get bigger by weight training or you can get smaller by weight training.

The answer to the charge of weirdness is the same answer one would give in any other line of work: some people are, some aren't. If you spend much time working out in weight rooms and gyms, you will meet individuals who build their muscles all winter in the gym so they can flex them all summer at the beach. If that strikes you as weird, so be it (it strikes us as sort of weird). It apparently does not strike the people who do it as weird. People like that are a small minority, but they represent the exaggeration of a perfectly legitimate reason for weight training, the desire to improve appearance (the same reason people get haircuts and shoeshines—or don't). On the other hand, the Kansas City Chiefs and other professional football teams that employ full-time strength coaches probably are not concerned about improving the teams' appearance, nor are the managements that pay their salaries. Obviously, their concern is the primary one. Weight training improves physical capacity. It improves your ability to play a sport or do a job, or just keep people from kicking sand on you at the beach. Again, we don't wish to oversimplify. People train with weights for all sorts of reasons. There is no doubt a concept of maleness involved in many instances (though women can use weights to advantage), but this is hardly the place for an extended discussion of machismo. Sufficient here to suggest that whatever reason you have for training with weights, it is adequate for you. You need not feel compelled to defend it.

The theory of weight lifting is simple enough: (1) *isolation* and (2) *intensification*. By isolating the muscles around the joints and exercising them intensively, you get results in an hour that you could not get in a week of sports activity. Weight-lifting equipment is designed to permit these two things.

The fundamental piece of equipment is the barbell. The bar normally has locks of one sort or another at each end permitting plates to be added and removed. York is probably the major name in weight-lifting equipment, but any set will do as long as it allows the weights to be balanced, interchanged and locked on. The bar must be able to sustain the weight (i.e., don't use a broomstick).

Barbells on a small scale are called dumbbells. One normally has a set of two, one for each hand. The above remarks about barbells apply equally to dumbbells. One caution: buy the same kind of dumbbells as barbells so the plates will fit interchangeably. Bars differ in diameter, and a set of plates for one kind of barbell may not fit another kind of dumbbell. Some fixed-weight dumbbells have irremovable plates. Therefore, since there is considerable expense in buying an entire set of all the various weights you need and unless you are very committed and quite well off, you would do better to purchase the adjustable ones—certainly, at least, to start.

In addition to a barbell and a set of dumbbells, a weight bench is desirable. It has a number of uses but is most frequently used for doing bench presses (p. 57). When buying

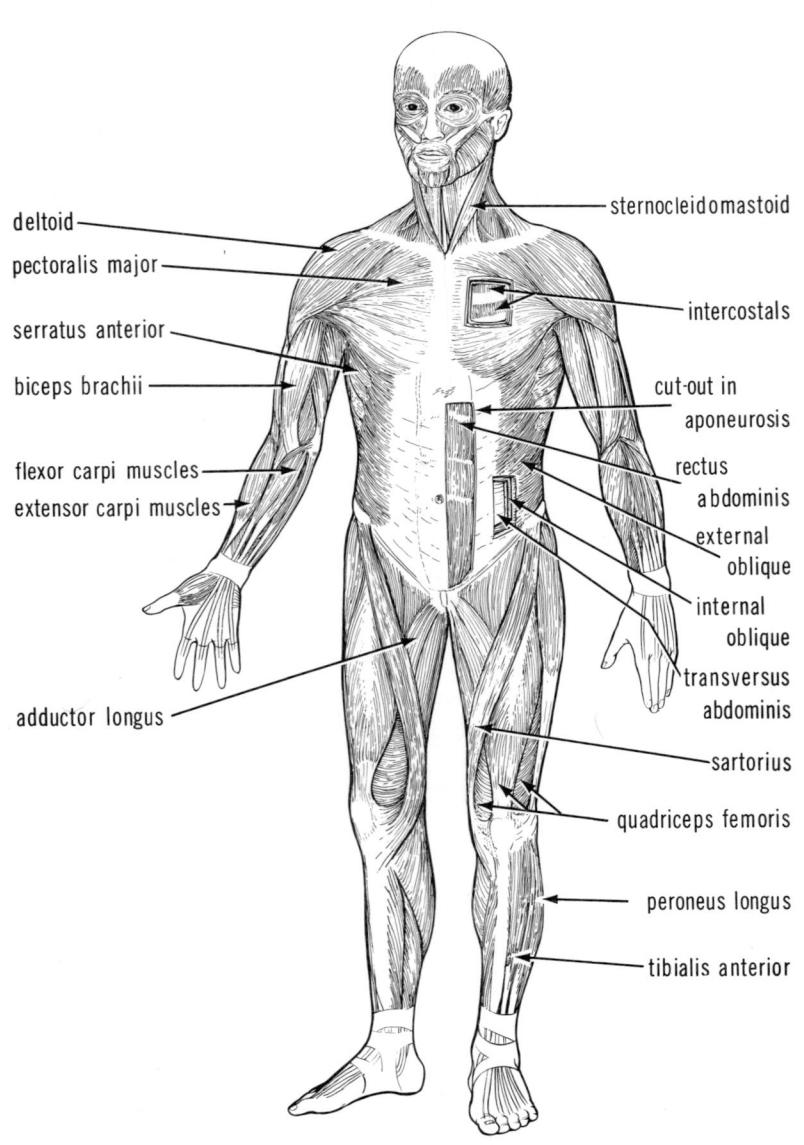

Body muscles: front view.

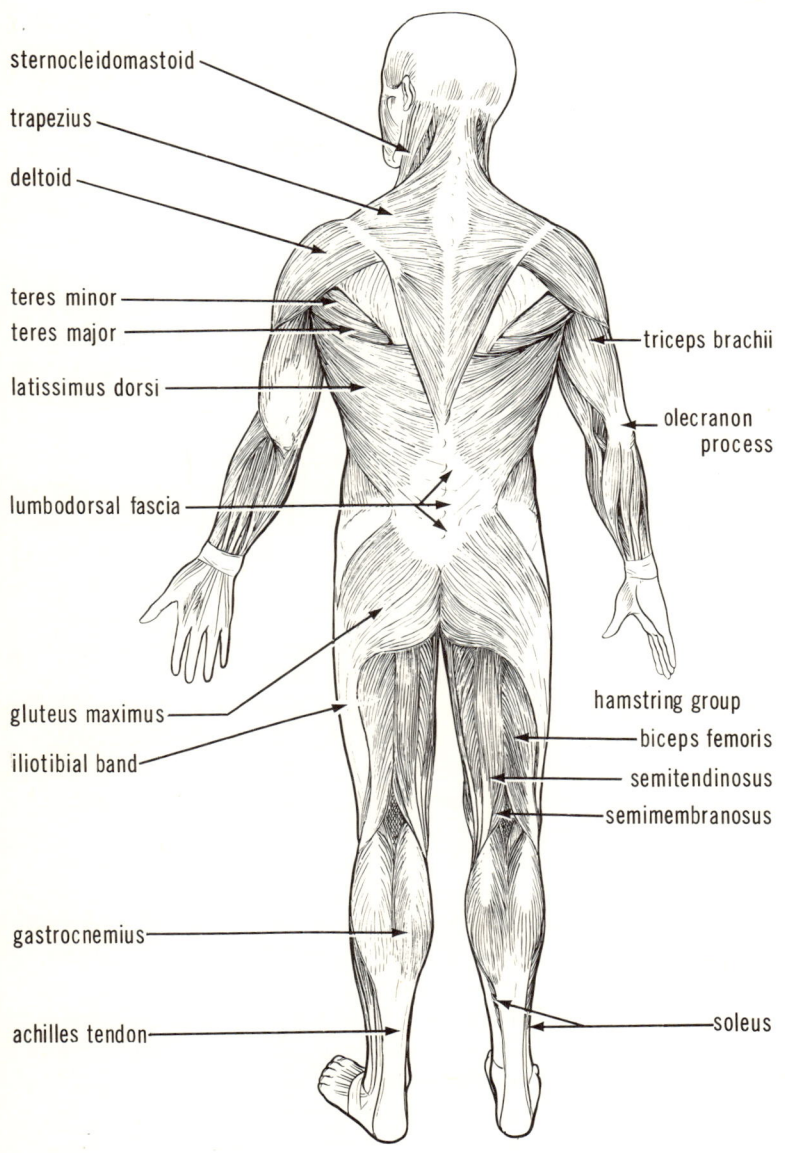

Body muscles: back view.

one, make sure it will support the weight you're lifting in addition to your own. (Most will support at least 250 pounds.) Some weight benches adjust into slant boards. This is a useful aspect, for it will enable you to do the exercises that call for a slant board (for example, incline presses, on p. 62).

There are a number of specialized items of equipment for specific exercises, such as a wrist-roll bar, weight boot, head harness and dip bars, that are best described in conjunction with the exercises employing them. But another type of exercise equipment should be mentioned here: the Circuit Trainer or Universal Gym. These are weight-training machines with an arrangement of weights on tracks or pulleys permitting you to do most of the exercises you can do with barbells, dumbbells and such. They are expensive. A 12-position Universal Gym will cost slightly under $3,000, and thus is rarely found in a private home. Schools, YMCAs and health clubs frequently have them. If you know how to exercise with conventional weights, it will take you very little time to figure out how to adjust to the Circuit Trainer. Since many readers will never encounter one, and those who do won't have any trouble with it, we'll not cover it in this book. But we would like to mention some advantages and disadvantages of such setups. There are a couple of advantages: (1) weight can be adjusted instantly for any exercise so that you waste no time changing plates, and (2) since all the weight is fixed, you can't drop it on yourself unless you are quite acrobatic. The disadvantages are less impressive: (1) some people contend that the balance is not true, and the weight is different from what it would be on a barbell (the writers have not found this to be the case); (2) advanced lifters complain that the Circuit Trainer does not permit a heavy enough lift (for example, most such devices have a maximum weight of 250 pounds on the bench press). Most readers of this book are not likely to worry terribly about that limit—not immediately, anyway.

We rather like the Circuit Trainer, and we think it is a

good idea for a person to work out in a gym, YMCA, health club or similar setup. The equipment is likely to be better (and safer) and more extensive than anything you would rig up at home, and other people will be working out in these places. You can watch them and learn from them. Everyone who works with weights copies others, and you should, too. No one objects. One word: if you join a health club, don't be caught up in the Victorian curlicues that usually ornament it. Vibrating belts, rollers, massages, steam baths, saunas, whirlpools and chrome plating on the dumbbells do not improve muscles. If you enjoy such things, enjoy them, but don't expect anything more from them.

Another minor advantage of working out with other people is that you'll learn the jargon and after a while will talk of pecs and lats and upper abs (abbreviations for muscle groups—we'll take them up in conjunction with the exercises). This won't increase your biceps, but it will make it easier to talk about weight training. Like any other endeavor, weight training has its own vocabulary. For convenience of reference, we'll define a couple of things: *reps* (repetitions) and *sets*. If, for example, you are doing a standing press (see p. 24), you will lift the barbell over your head and let it back down to your chest. That is 1 rep. If you do it 10 times, you have done 10 reps. If you then stop and rest, you will have done a set of 10 reps. If you do 10 more, stop and rest, and do 10 more, you will have done 3 sets of 10 reps each. You can do 3 sets of the same exercise in a row, or you can alternate sets: a set of presses, a set of curls (see p. 36), a set of presses, a set of curls, etc. Normally, one does 3 sets of each exercise (or more) at each workout. Obviously, doing all the exercises in this book would occupy you full time for the rest of your life. Since only you know what you are trying to accomplish, only you can work out the program you wish. If you are an athlete, it might be sensible to work it out with your coach.

And, finally, some *precepts:*

(1) Children under sixteen should check with the doctor before doing serious weight training. The joint connections in younger children are not fully formed, and certain kinds (not all kinds) of weight exercises can do some damage. Take this book to the doctor and ask him which exercises are okay.

(2) When lifting, control your breathing. You should be exhaling at the same time you strain. *Do not hold your breath.* This prevents a feeling of dizziness. Breathe in and, as you lift, breathe out.

(3) If you are going to train seriously with weights, you will need to control your tendency to worry about how you look to the other guy. Don't worry about how much he can lift compared to the weight you can lift. Otherwise, you will try to lift too much weight (to impress him). This will make you cheat on the exercise and consequently waste your time. Or you will avoid the exercises you can't do well; these are the ones you should concentrate on perfecting. All of us who work out want to keep up with the other guy, and you will, too. It has to do with being human, but it must be controlled. No matter how much you can lift, there will always be someone else who can lift more. In the words of a famous American philosopher, "never a horse that couldn't be rode; never a rider that couldn't be thrown."

(4) Heavy lifting (lots of weight and 5 to 10 reps) tends to build strength and size of muscle. Lighter lifting (less weight and more reps—over 10 reps) tends to build endurance and definition (tone) of muscle. Ideally, you may do both. What you concentrate on depends on your purpose. Generally, unless you have a specific reason for wishing to increase your size (you want to play defensive tackle; you want to increase your chest measurement so you'll look better in clothes), we are inclined to suggest lighter weights and more reps. There is no general advantage in being large.

(5) How much is light? How much is heavy? How many

reps should you do? There is no single answer to this. It depends on who is doing the lifting. Experiment with each exercise you choose to do until you find the maximum weight you can manage—that is, until you find the heaviest weight you can lift correctly for 10 reps. But don't cheat by swaying your back, twisting your shoulder into it, etc.; the body is very clever at trying to defeat your attempts to isolate muscles. Work at that weight until you can do 10 reps a set for 3 sets. Then add 5 pounds (or 10, depending on the exercise and you), and begin again. Or find the heaviest weight at which you can do 10 reps and add 5 pounds. Obviously, at some point you'll have to plateau, level off and stop adding weight.

(6) Give the muscles time to grow. Normally, you should do an exercise every other day. *Not* every day. Don't assume if 3 days a week is good, 7 days is better. It is not. Some people exercise several consecutive days, then rest several days. As you progress in all of this, you'll experiment and find what is best for you. Starting out, do the exercises only on alternate days. If you wish to work out every day, set up two programs. Do one program on Monday, Wednesday and Friday, and the other program on Tuesday, Thursday and Saturday. Rest on Sunday. On page 93 you will find a suggested program of training.

(7) Do the exercises properly. Don't cheat on them to get a little more weight up. It's like cheating at solitaire. Recognize what you can do properly, do that and be patient.

(8) Set yourself a schedule you can meet. Recognize how often you can work out, not how often you ought to be able to work out. If you aim too high and try to do too much, you'll end up doing nothing. Some is better than none. Three times a week is enough.

(9) Finally, while weight training is aimed primarily at improving muscles, light loads can also be used to increase the efficiency of the cardiovascular system (heart, lungs, arteries) provided little or no rest is taken between sets. But if you are truly serious about physical conditioning, you

will also do some aerobic exercises (running, swimming, bike riding, basketball, tennis—running is the best), and you will pay attention to what you eat. On page 95 you will find the titles of some books about physical conditioning that you should read. We hope you will.

But this book is concerned with weight training. In the pages to follow, we will describe and illustrate a variety of exercises with weights. Each chapter is devoted to a major area of the body (arms, back, legs and so forth). Within the chapters, the exercises are arranged, when appropriate, by subareas and muscle groups (ARMS: Biceps, Triceps, Forearms, Wrists, Hands). We have also listed the major sports for which such muscle development would be most appropriate.

This is a book for beginners. Advanced lifters won't suffer from having read it, but we are not primarily talking with people who lift competitively, who have been working out for years, who are in better shape than we are. Those of you, adults or children, who are starting out will find it hard going. No one ever wished weight training were harder. It is frequently dull and always tiring, but no matter what your age, the results are prompt and discernible. That is consolation, and perhaps all the consolation weight training offers.

1
Neck and Shoulders

NECK

Sports application: Football, wrestling, hockey, any contact sport.
Equipment needed: Head harness, bench.

Exercise 1: Neck Flexion. Lie on your back on a bench with your neck extended beyond the edge. Wearing a head harness (available at most sporting-goods stores, anywhere that barbells are sold) and a 5-pound barbell plate, start the exercise with your head at the same level or lower than the bench. Raise your head as far as possible, then lower it again. Three sets of 10.

Exercise 1: Neck Flexion.

Exercise 2: Neck Extension. Attach light weights to a head harness (start with 5 pounds and experiment). From a standing position, lean forward and bend your knees, resting your hands on them and keeping your arms straight. Your head is down, parallel to the floor. With a smooth, steady motion, lift head until you are looking straight ahead. Repeat. Three sets of 10.

Exercise 2: Neck Extension.

Exercise 3: Neck Bridge. Do this on a mat or rug if possible. Place a folded towel under your head as an added cushion. Lie flat on your back, pull your feet up close to your buttocks and comfortably apart (see illustration). Fold your arms across your chest; arch your body up into a bridge position (as shown). Let yourself back down slowly. Repeat. Three sets of 10. When the exercise becomes easy (if ever), hold a 10-pound weight on your chest when you do it. There are people who do pull overs and bench presses from the

Exercise 3: Neck Bridge.

bridge position, but they are unusual. Don't try that until your neck is well developed.

SHOULDERS

Sports application: Football, hockey, pole vaulting, wrestling, baseball (if one doesn't overdevelop so as to impede throwing), basketball (with same reservation as baseball), boxing.
Equipment needed: Barbells, dumbbells.

Exercise 1: Standing Press. This exercise puts a lot of stress on your lower back. If you have any back trouble, sit down to press. This is also one of those exercises that young children would do better to wait on. Now, if you still qualify, or want to, here's how: Grasp barbell with palms facing body and comfortably apart (as shown). Feet should be comfortably apart. Raise bar to chest, flipping palms back in process so that at chest level hands are facing out from body (this is easier to do than describe; see illustrations). Press bar over head. Return to chest level. Press up again and return. For a variation, lower the bar behind your neck. Three sets of 10 reps before adding 5 or 10 pounds. *Caution:* This is what most people think of when they think of weight lifting. Kids of all ages (including the writers of this book) are very much inclined to show off, to "see how much" they can lift. Consequently, kids of all ages are always trying to press more than they can and are getting hurt. Be sure you can handle the weight before you try to press it. Don't start too heavy. Start too light.

Exercise 1: Standing Press.

Exercise 2: Upright Rowing. Pick up barbell with hands spaced about 6 inches apart, palms in, knuckles facing away from body. Stand straight. Without shifting hands,

Exercise 2: Upright Rowing.

pull bar up to chin and lower to thigh level again. Begin with light weights. This is hard. Three sets of 10, then add 5 pounds.

Exercise 3: Bent-over Rowing. Stand with the trunk of the body in a horizontal position, with your legs slightly bent. Your arms are vertical while your hands grasp the bar with an overhand grip. Hand spacing is approximately 6 inches

Exercise 3: Bent-over Rowing.

wider than shoulder width. Flex your arms until the bar touches the chest. Then lower arms. Three sets of 10. Then add 5 pounds.

Exercise 4: Shrugs. Grasp barbell with hands comfortably spaced, about shoulder width. Allow barbell to hang at arms' length and shrug your shoulders up as far as you can. Try

Exercise 4: Shrugs.

to touch your ears with the points of your shoulders. You can begin fairly heavy on this one. But be sure to isolate the shoulders. Don't lurch or sway. Three sets of 10.

Exercise 5: Lateral Side Raises. Hold a set of light dumbbells at your side, palms in, knuckles out. Raise them simultaneously to a vertical position. Return. This is particularly useful for building the deltoid muscles that drape over the shoulder and extreme upper arm. Three sets of 10. Then add 5 pounds or less.

Exercise 5: Lateral Side Raises.

Exercise 6: Alternate Dumbbell Presses. As you might suspect, this exercise involves alternately pressing dumbbells. Hold a dumbell in each hand, at shoulder level (palms in, knuckles out). Press one and then the other alternately, returning each time to shoulder level. Keep your back straight. Three sets of 10 (each arm), then add 5 pounds.

Exercise 6: Alternate Dumbbell Presses.

2
Arms

UPPER-ARM BICEPS

Sports application: Football, wrestling, hockey, any sport where arm strength for pulling and grappling is important.
Equipment needed: A barbell, a chin-up bar, a dumbbell, a bench.

Exercise 1: Barbell Curls. Hold barbell as illustrated, palms out, elbows in close to the body, hands comfortably apart. Curl the bar up to the chin, using wrists and arms. Return it to the starting position. Don't sway; don't heave with your back. Isolate the biceps and make them do the work. If you can't do this without cheating, take off some weight. Three sets of 10. Then add 5 pounds.

Exercise 1: Barbell Curls.

Exercise 2: Reverse Curls. Use either dumbbells or a barbell. Hold bar palms down (the reverse of the barbell curl above), feet comfortably balanced. Curl bar up to chest. Be sure not to bow your elbows out. Return. Three sets of 10

Exercise 2: Reverse Curls.

reps before adding 5 pounds. This will be much harder than the barbell curl at first. Start with lighter weights.

Exercise 3: Chin-ups. Grasp bar (or handles on Universal Gym, as shown) with palms in toward body (not facing out; that's for different muscles), as shown. Pull yourself up to chin over the bar. Drop back down (all the way). Do 3 sets. When you are able to do 3 sets of 10, then you can increase weight by wearing a weight belt, by tying a plate around your waist with rope, or you can ask someone to place a dumbbell in the crook of your knees. Adding weight is not, however, for beginners. It is never necessary.

Exercise 3: Chin-ups.

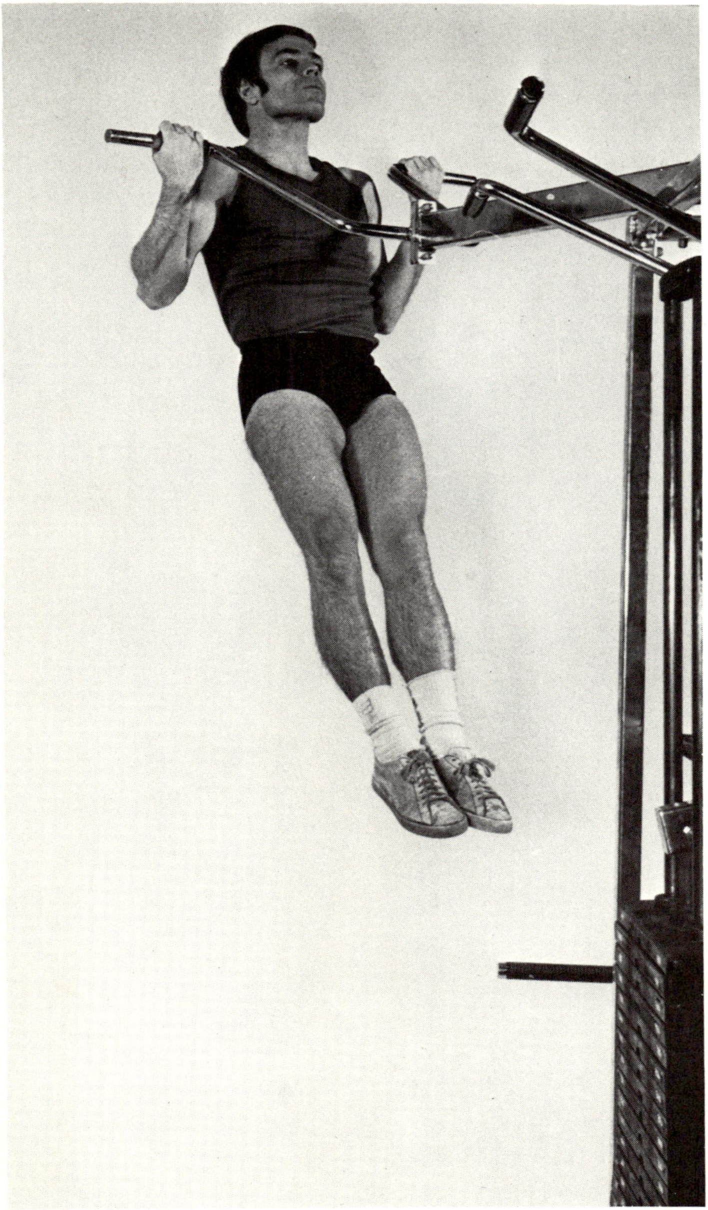

Exercise 4: Dumbbell Curls. Hold a dumbbell in each hand, palms facing each other. Curl to chin and return. Alternate

Exercise 4: Dumbbell Curls.

arms for each rep of this exercise. This thickens the whole upper arm, not just the biceps. Three sets of 10.

Exercise 5: Concentration Curls. Sit down (as shown). Lean forward, bracing elbow against thigh. Curl the dumbbell up to the chin (don't move your chin down to it) and return. Three sets of 10 before adding 5 pounds.

Exercise 4: Concentration Curls.

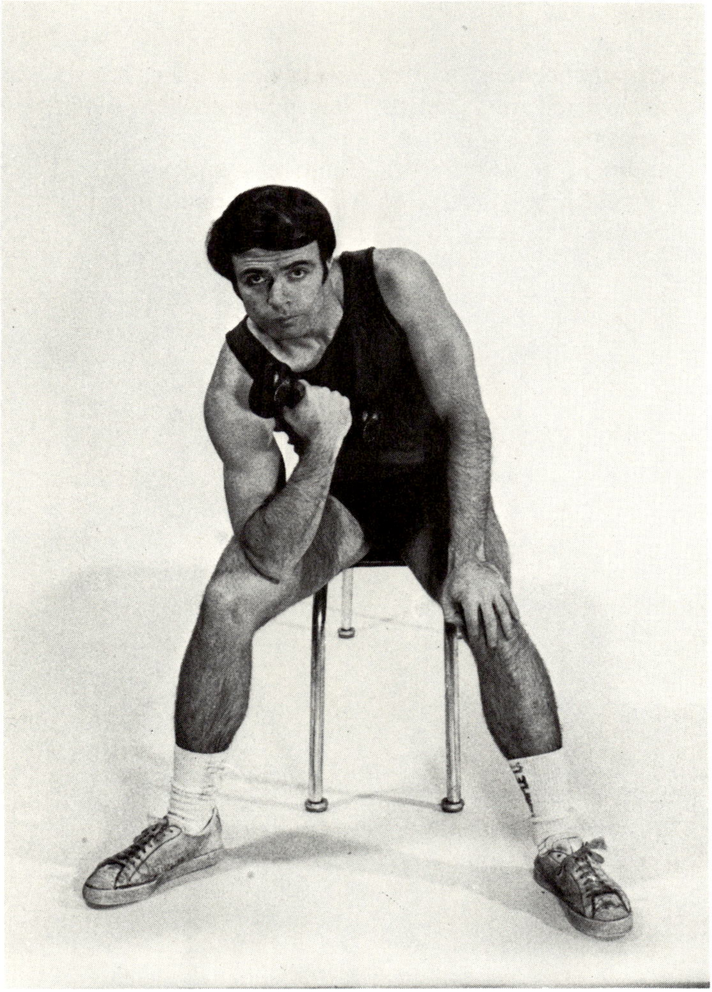

UPPER-ARM TRICEPS

Sports application: Football, wrestling, hockey, boxing, any sport where arm strength for pushing and shoving is important.

Equipment needed: Barbell, dumbbells, pulley-weight device or lat machine (a piece of equipment found in most gymnasiums), dip bars.

Exercise 1: Pulley Press Down.

Exercise 1: Pulley Press Down. Using a pulley-weight device or lat machine, place hands close together on the bar, palms toward floor, and push bar down, extending arms fully. Let bar return about as high as your solar plexus and push it down again. Be careful to do it with the arms and not the back and shoulders. Three sets of 10 reps before adding 5 pounds.

Exercise 2: Triceps Extension. Use a light dumbbell. If it's too heavy, you'll hurt your elbow and shoulder. You'll also cheat on the exercise. Raise dumbbell over the head (as shown) and, keeping upper arm stationary while bending elbow, lower dumbbell behind neck. Raise it to vertical again. Three sets of 10 reps before adding 5 pounds.

Exercise 2: Triceps Extension.

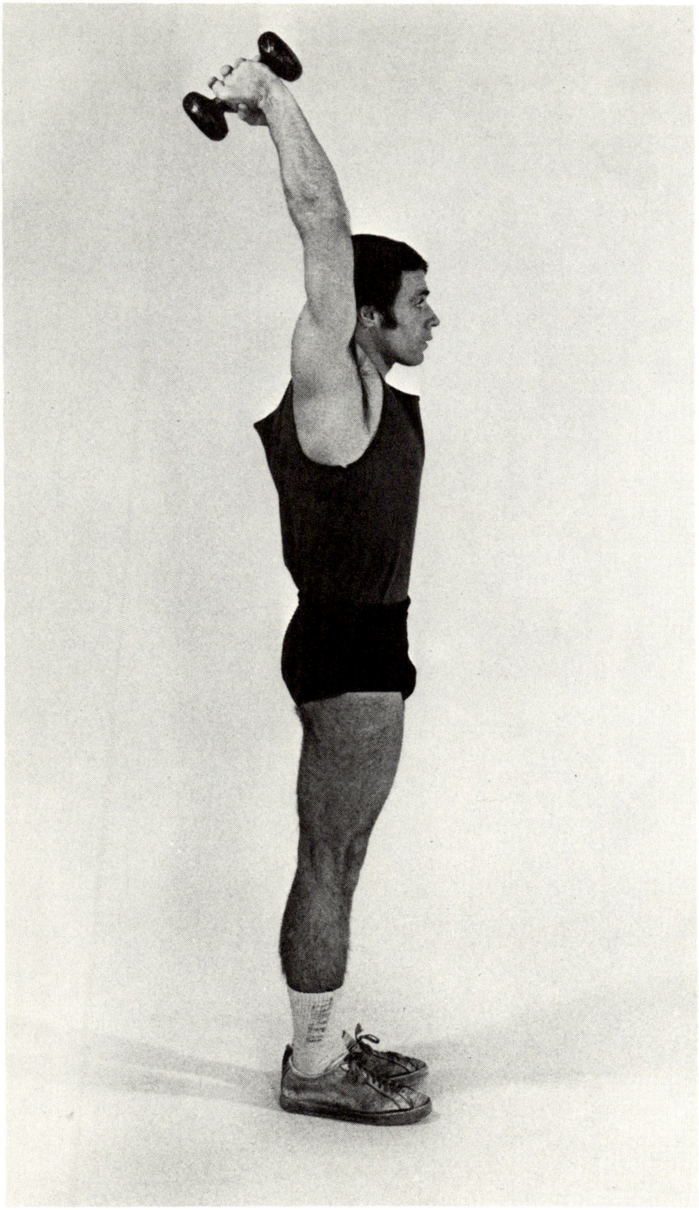

Exercise 3: Bent-arm Pull Overs. Lie on your back on the bench. Grasp barbell shoulder width apart and raise it to your chest. Try to keep your elbows in to reduce the strain on them.

Exercise 3: Bent-arm Pull Overs.

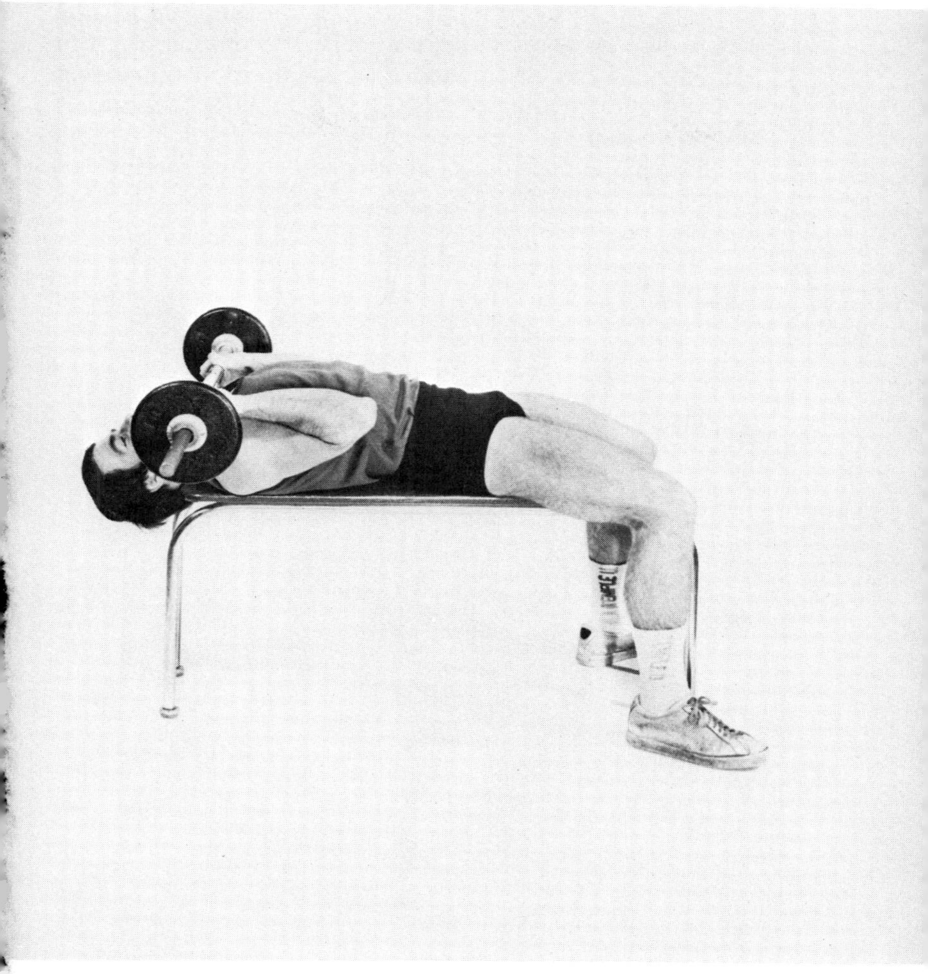

Exercise 4: Dips. These are essentially push-ups on parallel bars or dip bars, as shown, and may be done on any two stationary objects that permit it. Don't do it on things that will slide out from under you (like the backs of two straight chairs). Grasp bars (as shown), and jump up and forward so that your straight arms are carrying all your weight and your feet are off the floor (bend them up if the bars are too low). Let yourself down as far as you can go, then push

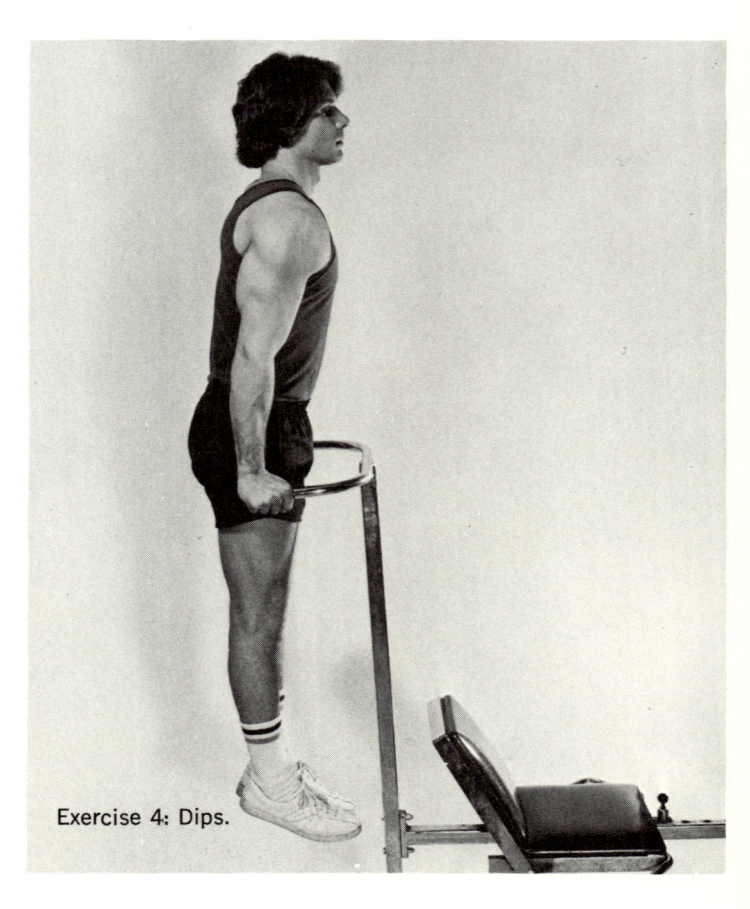

Exercise 4: Dips.

yourself back up. (You won't be able to let yourself down very far or do very many reps at first. But this is an exercise in which you make very rapid advances, so be of good cheer and do what you can.) Do 3 sets. When you are able to do 3 sets sets of 10, you can add more weight in the same way you could for chin-ups (p. 40), though here, as there, you needn't. This exercise is also good for chest development.

FOREARMS, WRISTS, HANDS

Sports application: Wrestling, boxing, football, any sport requiring hand strength (e.g., a defensive end who must hand-fight blockers). Also, sports like hockey, baseball and tennis where forearms and wrists must be strong and quick.
Equipment needed: Barbell, a roll-up bar.

Exercise 1: Wrist Curls.

Exercise 1: Wrist Curls. Use *light* weights for this. Use a barbell. Sit down. Grasp bar as you did for barbell curls (p. 36). With hands extended just beyond knees, and forearms on thighs, curl the bar up with your wrists (as shown). Do not move forearms. Don't rock. Return bar to starting position. Repeat. Then reverse hands and do reverse wrist curls. Alternate until you've done 3 sets of each, 10 reps. Then add 5 pounds. The reverse wrist curls can pull some tendons if you put on too much weight.

Exercise 2: Wrist Roll Ups. Circuit Trainers usually have a wrist-roll device. If you are not on a Circuit Trainer, you can make your own wrist roll up. Get a thick length of wood or pipe (the sawed-off upper end of a broken baseball bat is good, i.e., the fat end, not the handle.) Attach a rope or chain to the middle of it. Attach weight to the other end. Hold arms straight down in front of you, palms in toward body, and roll weight up and down. Alternate rolling the weight up by turning the hands toward you and turning the hands away from you (always with palms down; see illustration). Do 3 sets of 10 reps and then add 5 pounds.

Exercise 2: Wrist Roll Ups.

3
Chest

Sports application: Chest exercises are very useful for increasing chest cavity and lung capacity. Chest exercises also are important for getting bigger. Heavy bench presses, for example, can increase your upper body size from a size 40 to a size 46 in a couple of years. This is important to remember not only by those people who want to grow larger for a sport like football, but for those people who do not want to bet bigger. For people who are *not* trying to develop size, it is a better idea to do many reps with light weights or 1 or 2 reps with heavy loads.

Equipment needed: A bench (preferably with weight rests), barbell, dumbbells, parallel bars, slant board.

Exercise 1: Bench Press. Lie on your back on a bench, legs straddled, feet on floor. Space hands about shoulder width on the bar, palms facing away from you, arms vertical. Lower bar down from rack to chest and push it straight up to arms' length. Return it to chest and push it up again. Breathe in as weight comes down to your chest; breathe out as you press weight up. Don't arch your back; don't bounce the weight

Exercise 1: Bench Press.

on your chest. Breathe properly. Return the weight to the rack when you're through. Do 3 sets of 8 to 12 reps each. If the bench doesn't have a rack, have someone hand you the weight, act as a spotter and take it from you when you finish. You can do this exercise lying on the floor, but you will not get as much from it because you will be unable to lower it as far. Thus, the inner pectoral muscles won't develop.

Exercise 2: Lateral Raise, Lying. Lie on your back on the bench. Take a dumbbell in each hand, palms in toward the body. Bend your elbows comfortably (*do not keep your arms straight*). Start with the weights at bench level. Raise them above your chest as shown. Lower again to bench level. Breathe as you do for bench presses (in while lowering, out while raising). Do 3 sets of 10 each. When you do 15 reps, add 5 pounds.

Exercise 2: Lateral Raise, Lying.

Exercise 3: Varied Push-ups. Once you've been lifting for a while, you'll be able to grind out many standard push-ups. To make them more useful, have someone put a 10- to 25-pound barbell plate on your back and do push-ups that way. You can also try doing the push-ups on your fingertips, or between two benches. Before you get this exotic, of course, make sure you can do the standard push-ups (say, 3 sets of 25).

Exercise 3: Varied Push-ups.

Exercise 4: Dips. See same exercise in Chapter 2, p. 52.

Exercise 5: Incline Press. This exercise fills out the upper pectoral muscles. Lie on your back on a slant board. Grasp a barbell with your hands about shoulder width apart, palms out, and press it straight up (toward the sky, not out from

Exercise 5: Incline Press.

the chest). Return it to shoulder level. Three sets of 10 or 12 reps. You can do the same exercise with dumbbells. If you use dumbbells, hold them palms in.

Exercise 6: Straight-arm Pull Over. Be sure to use light weight on this exercise. Too heavy a weight will strain the shoulder joints. Lie on your back on the bench. Grasp barbell in the middle, hands comfortably spaced. Raise barbell

Exercise 6: Straight-arm Pull Over.

straight up and lower it at arms' length behind you. Bring it back to vertical-arms position. Repeat. Don't bend your elbows. Inhale as you lower weight. Exhale as you raise it. Three sets of 15 reps.

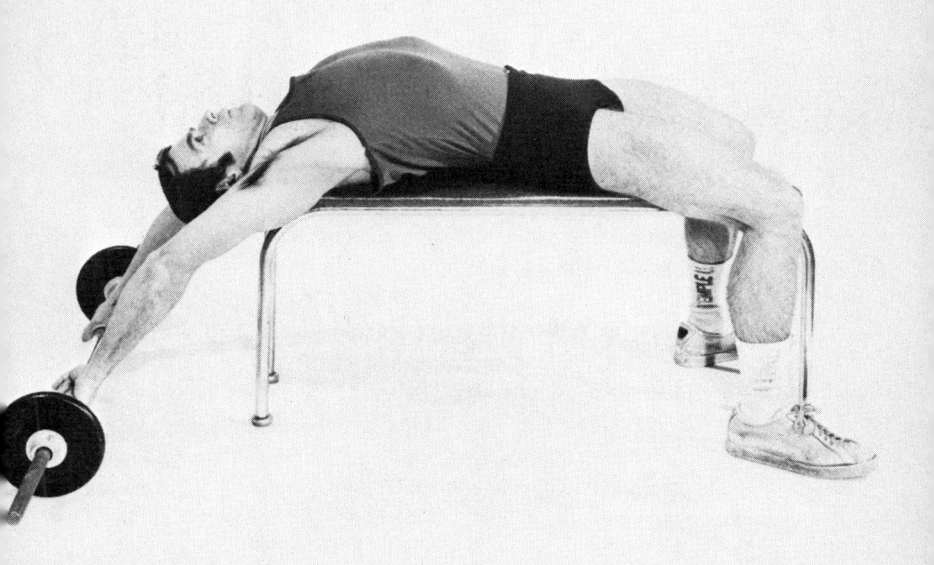

4
Back

Sports application: Football, pole vaulting, wrestling, swimming, baseball, any event needing strength of back and shoulders.

Equipment needed: A pulley device or lat machine, barbell, dumbbells, chin-up bar.

Exercise 1: Wide-arm Pull Down. Grasp the pull-down bar at the ends, palms facing away from body. Pull bar down behind neck all the way, raise to full extent of arms. Do 3 sets of 10 or 12. This helps build not only the latissimus dorsi (hence the name lat machine) but the pectoral muscles and biceps as well. A good exercise.

Exercise 1: Wide-arm Pull Down.

Exercise 2: Bent-over Rowing. See p. 28. This exercise develops both shoulder and upper-back muscles.

Exercise 3: Bent-over Lateral Raises. Bend at the waist, with body roughly parallel to the floor and knees straight or slightly flexed. Grasp a dumbbell in each hand, palms in toward body. Extend your arms out from your body and

Exercise 3: Bent-over Lateral Raises.

raise the weight to shoulder level. Return the weight to the floor. The motion is as if you were trying to fly (the exercises made with this kind of motion are often called flies). Don't sway or buck the weight up. Don't rest the weights on the floor. Do 3 sets of 10 or 12. In addition to the other muscles of back and shoulder, this helps the teres major and teres minor.

Exercise 4: Wide-grip Chin-ups. This differs in two basic respects from the chin-ups in Chapter 2. (1) The grip is reversed; you take hold of the chin-up bar with the palms facing away from the body. (2) The grip is wide, as wide as the bar (and your reach) permit. Pull yourself chin up over the bar. Alternate by pulling yourself up until you can

Exercise 4: Wide-grip Chin-ups.

touch the back of your neck to the bar. Let yourself down full-length each time. Do 3 sets. When you are able to do 3 sets of 10, you can add weight (as in previous chin-up exercises and dips—though you need not) if you become expert.

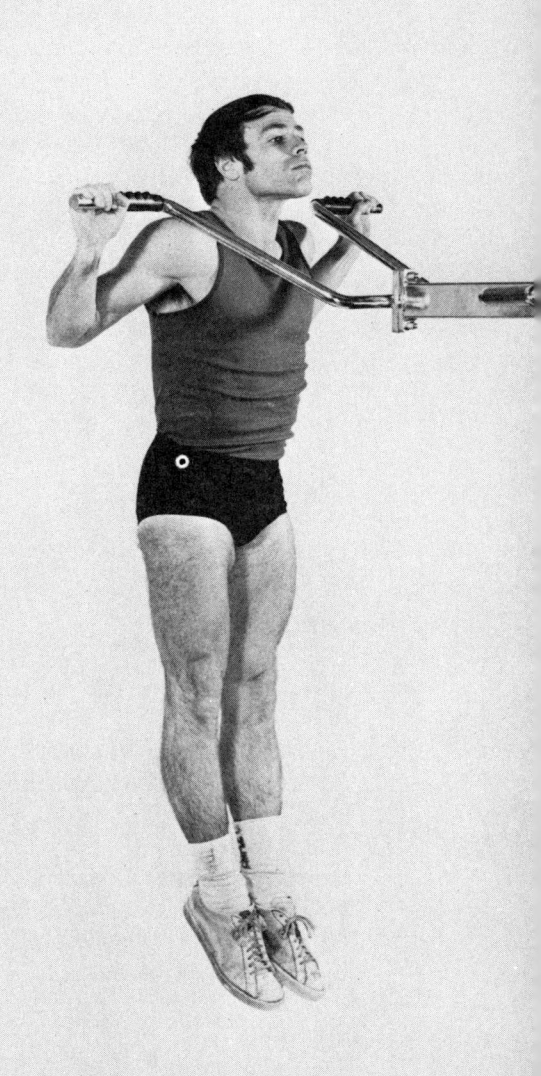

5
Waist

ABDOMEN

Sports application: All participants in sports need a strong stomach and lower trunk, especially for football, hockey, wrestling, lacrosse, boxing, diving.
Equipment needed: A bench, a chin-up bar, an incline board.

Exercise 1: Leg Raises. Lie on your back on the bench. Hold onto each side. With legs straight, raise them to about 45 degrees. Then lower them to the bench. Repeat. Work up to 30 or 40 of these.

Exercise 1: Leg Raises.

Exercise 2: Hanging Leg Lifts. This is not as macabre as it sounds. Begin by hanging at arms' length from a chin-up bar. With your legs straight, raise them to 90 degrees so that your body forms a kind of L. Lower them. Repeat. Don't swing. Work up to 30 or 40 of these.

Exercise 2: Hanging Leg Lifts.

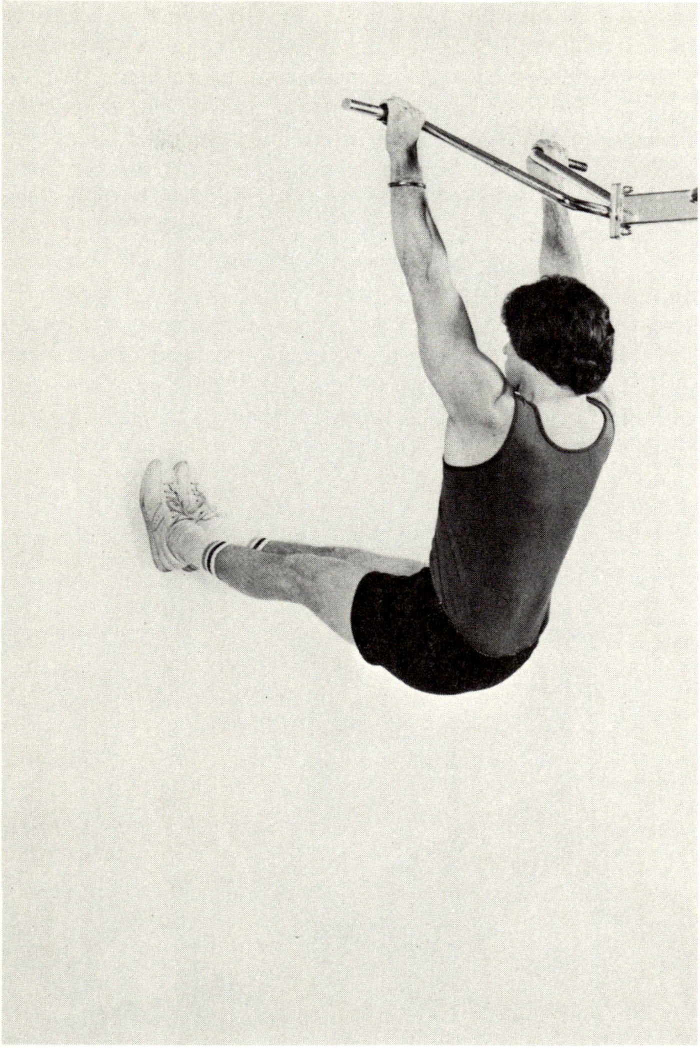

Exercise 3: Sit-ups. Lie flat on your back on the floor—or on an abdominal board with footholds, if one is available—with your knees bent. (Yes, with your knees bent. It takes the strain off your lower back and it isolates the abdominal muscles.) Sit up and touch your elbows to your knees and return. If you have trouble keeping your feet on the floor, you may secure them by locking them under a barbell. This exercise should be done with the hands clasped behind the back of the head, but if you find this difficult, you can start out with your hands more forward—say, cupped behind each ear or pressed against your forehead or folded on your chest, or, if you must, reaching out ahead of you. The further forward your arms, the easier the sit-up. Once you are able to do sit-ups like this with your hands behind your head, work up to 30 or 40 reps.

Exercise 3: Sit-ups.

Exercise 4: Incline Sit-ups (not illustrated). These are simply sit-ups done on an incline. What you need is a board that has a foothold. Ideally, it should be adjustable so that the pitch can be increased or decreased. Lie on the board with your head lower than your feet. Do sit-ups the same way. A variation is to lie with the head higher than the feet and, grasping the board or the foothold, raise the legs up all the way over the head and return. In either case, the incline simply increases the stress and gets more exercise into the movement. Thirty or 40 reps of either.

OBLIQUES

Sports application: Same as abdomen.
Equipment needed: Barbell or dumbbells, incline board.

Exercise 1: Side Bends. Hold a light dumbbell in one hand. Stand upright and bend your body to the right as if you were trying to touch the outside of your knee with the dumbbell. Straighten, bend to the opposite side. Repeat, holding dumbbell in other hand. Do 50 or 100 of these. Do all your bending sideways, not forward or back. *Caution:* Not everyone (including the writers) agree on the effect of these exercises. Some say that many repetitions with light

Exercise 1: Side Bends.

weight will help slim the waist. Others contend that even light reps will eventually enlarge the obliques and thicken your waist. Still others claim these should only be done with no weights at all. Your best bet is to experiment a bit. The exercise will strengthen the external and internal oblique muscles, that is certain. But whether it will make your waist smaller is unsettled. Most of us are not interested in making the waist bigger.

Exercise 2: Side Sit-ups. For this exercise you'll need something to hook your feet under. If you have an abdominal board with footholds, that is ideal. If not, you might hook your feet under a heavy barbell, or have someone hold your ankles. Lie on your side, hands behind head, and bend your body up sideways as if trying to touch your elbow to the outside of your knee. Repeat. Work up to 30 or 40 reps on each side.

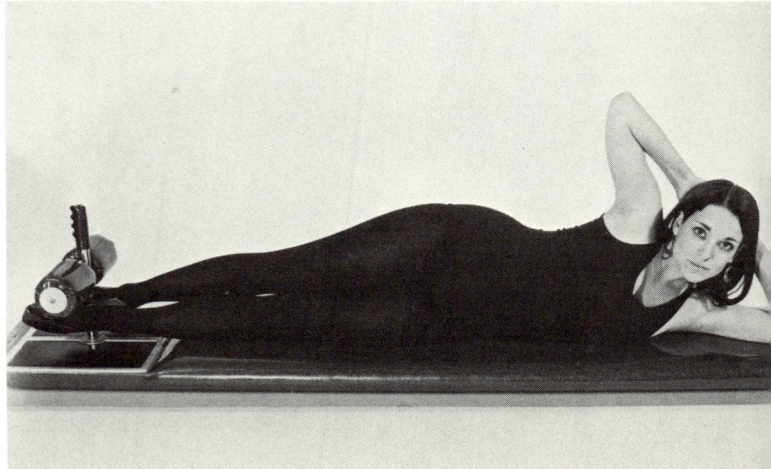

Exercise 2: Side Sit-ups.

6
Legs

THIGHS

Sports application: Football, basketball, hockey, swimming and any sport requiring leg power.

Equipment needed: A 2×4 board, a bench, barbell, weight boot, a thigh-and-knee machine if possible.

Exercise 1: Half Squat. Don't do a full squat. Full squats place too severe a strain on the knee joints. Stand erect and hold a light barbell across your shoulders behind your neck. Place heels on a 2×4. Squat slowly till thighs are about parallel to the floor. Go back up again to a position just short of knee lock (to keep tension on thighs). Repeat. Inhale when going down. Exhale when going up. It is a good idea to put a bench, or chair, behind you so that when you reach the half-squat position your buttocks will hit the bench and you can't go down too far. Spotters are helpful to assist you if you lose your balance. Do not, however, sit on the bench. Three sets of 10 reps.

Exercise 1: Half Squat.

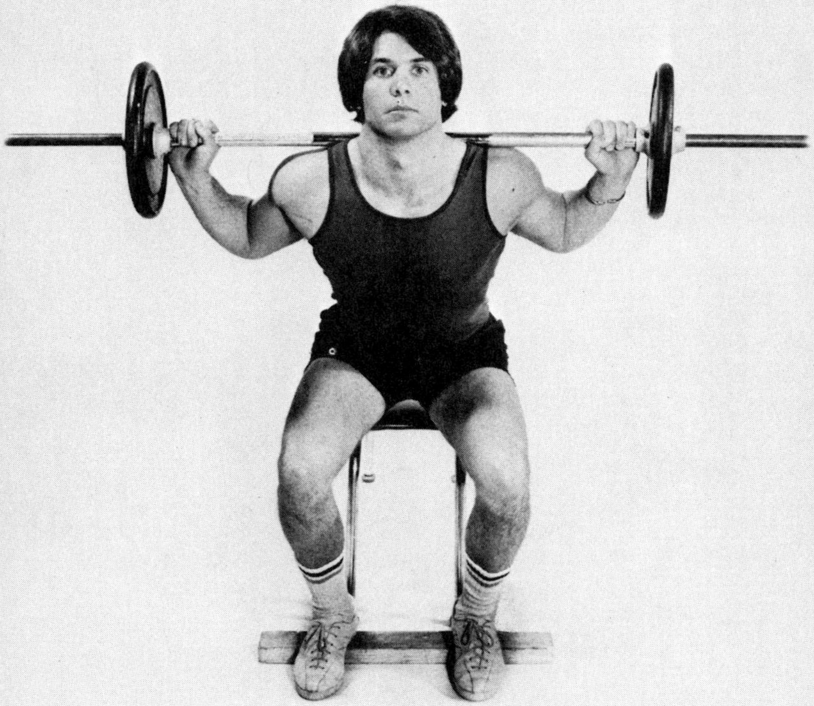

Exercise 2: Thigh Extension. Use a thigh-and-knee machine if one is available. Sit on the end of the bench and hook your feet under the weights, as shown. Hold the edges of the bench and, by extending the knees, raise your legs so that they are parallel to the floor; let them down slowly. Three sets of 10 to 12 reps. If you do not have access to

Exercise 2: Thigh Extension.

this piece of equipment, you may use a weight boot or improvise by taping a plate to an old shoe. With the weight boot on one foot and a rolled-up towel under the knee of the same leg, do the exercise as described above; then put the boot on the other foot and repeat.

Exercise 3: Reverse Leg Raise. Use a thigh-and-knee machine if one is handy. (Again, a weight boot will do, but be sure to exercise both legs equally.) Lie prone and hold onto the bench. Lift your feet behind you and try to touch

Exercise 3: Reverse Leg Raise.

your buttocks with your heels. Then lower slowly and repeat. Three sets of 12 reps. This builds the muscles in the back of the thigh and the buttocks.

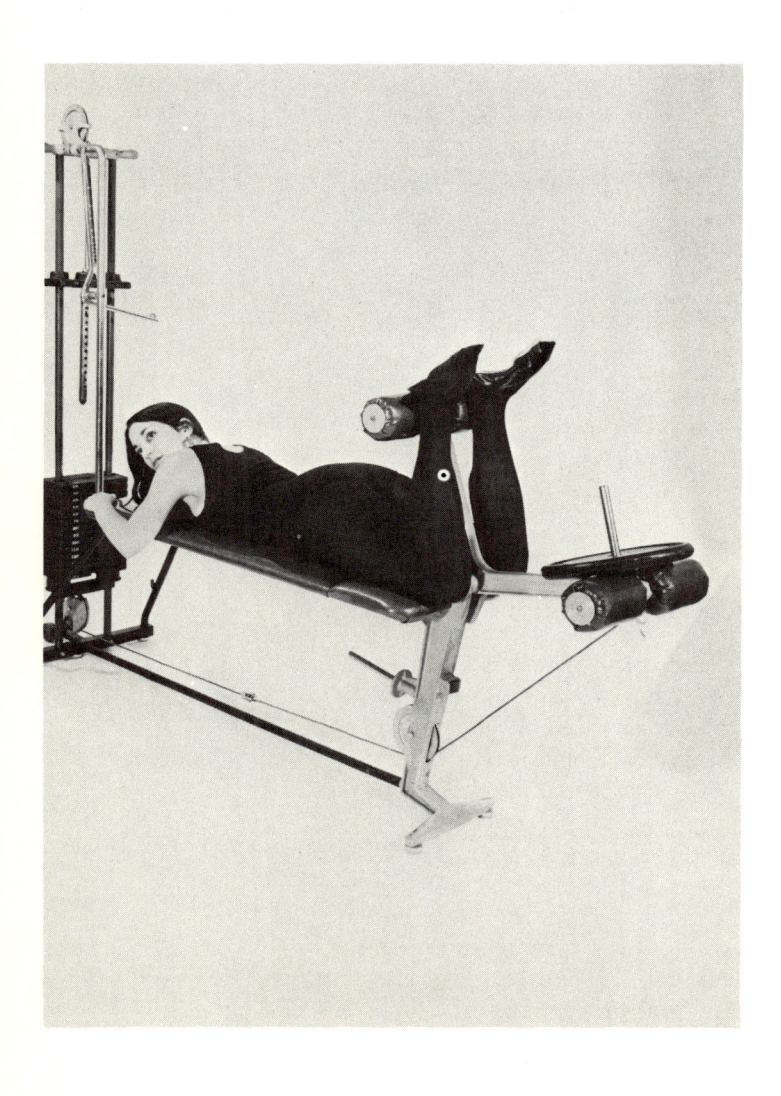

CALVES

Sports application: Track, basketball, baseball, football, diving.
Equipment needed: Barbell, 2×4, dumbbell.

Exercise 1: Calf Raises.

Exercise 1: Calf Raises. Stand erect with heavy barbell resting behind your neck on your shoulders. It is easier to maintain your balance if you lean against a wall. Place balls of feet, comfortably apart, on a 2×4. With your back straight and without bending your legs, rise up on your toes, and back down. Three sets of 12 reps.

Exercise 2: One-legged Calf Raise. With a dumbbell in one hand, stand with the ball of your foot on a barbell plate or a 2×4. If the dumbbell is in your right hand, stand

Exercise 2: One-legged Calf Raise.

on your right foot or vice versa. Support yourself with your other hand against a wall. Rise up on your toes. Three sets of 10 reps for each leg.

7
Training Programs for the Beginning Lifter

Now that you are familiar with the weight-training exercises, you should put together a program of training. Begin with about 7 to 8 lifts and select them so that the entire body musculature will be exercised. Here is a basic program for a person wanting to improve both his appearance and the condition of his skeletal muscles:

> Barbell Curl
> Bench Press
> Upright Rowing
> Bent-over Rowing
> Sit-up
> Standing Press
> Half Squat

After about 2 to 3 months of training, more lifts may be

added depending on your purpose for exercising. If you are interested in more strength and muscle size in your arms, then add the dumbbell curl and triceps-extension lifts. Maybe you are more concerned about developing the legs. If so, add calf raises and thigh-extension lifts. Perhaps you want to shape up the waistline area; then add leg raises and side bends. Be sure that you do not add too many lifts—or too soon. Your body needs time to get adjusted to the extra work. As a rule of thumb, don't add more exercises if you feel overly tired after a workout and, in particular, during the next training session. If you do feel exhausted, then slack off a bit until your muscles get in better shape.

If for some reason you are not able to train long enough during one session to complete all the lifts, try exercising the upper body for 3 days and the abdominal and leg muscles on 2 or 3 other days a week. Just make sure you don't exercise the same body parts on successive days. The following is a typical split program:

Monday, Wednesday and *Friday*
Barbell Curl
Bench Press
Upright Rowing
Bent-over Rowing
Standing Press

Tuesday and *Thursday*
Sit-up
Half Squat

Weight training may be used to develop endurance of the muscles, the heart and the circulatory system, but special training is necessary in terms of the weights handled. Using the same exercise program described above, select a weight for each lift which is 40 percent of the maximum weight you can lift. Then perform 10 reps with each lift, going from one lift to another with only a few seconds' rest between exercises. Make sure you alternate the exercises so that the same body parts are not worked in succession. By doing this, you will be able to continue exercising until all the lifts are completed for 2 or 3 sets. The following sequence is suggested:

1. Barbell Curl
2. Bench Press
3. Sit-up
4. Upright Rowing
5. Standing Press
6. Bent-over Rowing
7. Half Squat

An Afterword on Physical Condition

There is little argument that being in good physical condition is better than not being in good physical condition. Weight training, as we said in the Introduction, is only one phase of getting into good shape. It is not the most important aspect of conditioning, though its results are the most impressive. Proper diet and proper cardiovascular exercise are both of more importance. The best book on nutrition and health that we know is Jean Mayer's *Overweight*, (Prentice-Hall, Englewood Cliffs, N.J.). Dr. Mayer is a professor of nutrition at Harvard and one of the world's leading authorities in the nutritional sciences. The topic of diet attracts more semiliterate quacks than any other subject. Dr. Mayer is a voice of sane intelligence in the midst of babble. The best book we know on the cardiovascular condition is Kenneth Cooper's *Aerobics*, (available in paperback from Bantam Books, New York). His training program and point system are founded on solid research, and they work. In addition, to keep track of developments in the field, read *Strength and Health,* a magazine devoted to body building. This publication appears regularly and, aside from its idolatrous approach to Mr. America types, is reasonably reliable and often contains good suggestions.

If you are going to start working out, especially if you are adult (or of middle age), get a physical. When you begin, go easy. It is better to go too slowly, not too quickly. Don't believe all the mythology that fogs up the locker room in every gym in the country. One of the authors of this book began running regularly at age thirty-eight. When he began, he walked a lap and ran a lap on a track that was 11 laps to the mile. In 6 months, he was jogging 6 miles, and now does 10 to 15 miles a week without great discomfort (though not without some discomfort—no one ever promised you a rose garden). We both know a man who at thirty-five started to do bench presses with 90 pounds. In a year, he was up to 220. It works, if you do it right. And there's no hurry. If you are not in shape by this Monday, you'll be in shape next Monday, or five Mondays from now—if you're faithful to yourself and do what we've told you.

But what we've told you is only the basis for experimentation. As you go on, you'll work out your own program for your needs. You'll discover exercises that suit your temperament, strength, circumstances and need. "We are fed," Ralph Waldo Emerson once said, "not that we may eat, but that we may work."